LOVE IS IN THE AIR

Henry H. Petersohn

Guys look for gals - gals look for guys. That attraction is built into everyone's genes but the process can take a lot of time and have many disappointments along the way. Once a couple find each other, a new joint life begins. Happiness, however, depends on more than just joining hands and moving in together.

What the guy may be expecting;

A. A willing sex partner.

B. A soft voice in his ear.

C. A clean and sweet-smelling companion.

D. An interested listener.

E. Some sensible responses to his questions or concerns.

F. A clean bathroom.

G. No stockings hanging from the shower bar.

H. Suits cleaned and pressed.

I. She does the laundry.

J. She puts the clean clothes in his dresser;

K. She sets the table and serves meals

L. He gets meals when he wants with things he likes.

M. She does all the shopping for food.

N. She is a good driver.

O. She understands and supports his interests in sports.

P. She likes his ideas about vacations, travel, and visiting family.

Q. She is willing to let him manage their finances.

R. She agrees with him about having a family and when.

S. She agrees with him about where to live and the furnishings he wants.

What the gal may be expecting:

A. A kind and tender lover.

B. A pleasant voice in her ear and a smile on his face.

C. A clean and sweet-smelling companion.

D. An avid listener.

E. Sensible responses to her questions and concerns.

F. A clean bathroom.

G. She can hang stockings or a slip to dry on the shower bar or a towel bar without objections.

H. He takes his suits and pants to the cleaner when they need it and has them sew up loose seams or hems.

I. He puts dirty clothes in the washer and when clean puts them into a dryer and then back in the drawer.

J. He is a careful driver and agrees on when to leave the house and where to go. If there are alternate routes, he willingly takes suggestions from her.

K. He will help prepare salads, clean veggies, cut meats, chicken etc. for eating and put them on the table. In many cases, he can be a great cook, will do some of the cooking and makes things she likes.

L. He helps set the table and willingly brings food items to the table.

M. He understands her interests in cooking, baking, and doing needlework

N. He listens to her suggestions and requests to entertain at home as well as go out as a couple or with friends. If he is concerned with the size, costs. Who gets invited, what they will serve or the proposed conversation topics, he will let her know in advance.

O. He is appreciative of and fosters her interests in sports and social activities.

P. He consults her interests and feelings when planning vacations, travel and visiting family.

Q. He listens to her suggestions for managing family finances.

R. He pays attention to her concerns about starting a family and when.

S. He pays attention to her suggestions on where to live and the furnishings they need.

Conflicts take the joy out of marriage. A happy marriage is what both parties want but they each have different expectations. Both the guy and the gal will have to think about how important an item is. He needs to create a list of items he expects to have. She needs her own list of items she would like to have in the marriage. Then he sits down and rates all the items on his list as being very important, important, negotiable or trivial. She sits down and creates her own list of items she wants in the marriage. Since tastes and expectations change over time, some of the items could turn out to be more or less important in the next year. Now is the time for both to stop for a few minutes to have some coffee or tea and perhaps a piece of cake and chat about how some of the items on the two lists could actually fit together. This can be a very nice few minutes without anybody else looking over your shoulder and telling you what to do.

What about meals at home? Of course, you will often go out but the comfort, quality and variety of meals at home you can have with a loved one is hard to beat. Many couples like to share the meal preparation and serving, and the opportunity to talk on any subject. Frequently, a guy will find great pleasure in being a chef in his own home and is not hesitant in preparing plain and fancy dinners to please his palate and his gal. Some chaps are natural chefs and have a special talent in preparing soup, seafood, meats, desserts, etc. Later, with a family, there is great fun for him as he prepares a special cake or perhaps cherries jubilee for a birthday

When children come along, some fathers hesitate in first picking up a baby but when the infant smiles and then reaches out and grasps his finger he is truly happy at having this new one to share with his gal.

But life is not all peaches and cream. Although there can be many happy occasions, there are many problems to cope with as your infant grows older. He will need clothes, medical care, education and guidance on many different issues so parents must develop a sense of humor and get sensible advice on raising their children so everyone in the family are happy.

NEGOTIATE THE DIFFERENCES IN LIVING TOGETHER

Now be realistic. Probably one of the first thing to discuss is the bathroom. Is there any compelling reason for either of you to throw towels or clothes on the floor? Get a good-sized hamper and put the laundry items in it. If the guy is rushing to get to work, the gal can dump the contents in the washer and turn it on. On his day at home, he can do this. Sharing this necessary chore is a reasonable action. It avoids making his gal play the role of a full-time maid which is demeaning.

Each one will have some expectations for what he/she should do in their love nest to make it their idea of paradise. Each one needs to write down a list of what they expect from the other. There will be many items which are almost immediately agreeable Others need some discussion to get a happy agreement. Here are some major topics to cover.

<u>Travel and a Honeymoon</u>: Marriage details are often left to the bride's family. After the wedding where do you want to go, what do you two want to see? How long will you be away? Extensive travel may mean you want to check options with AA A or a travel agent.

Local walking or hiking is easy. Bicycles or a car are very convenient. A railroad, bus, airplane or ship can take you long distances. Do you need or want to go on a formal tour? How long will you be away from home? Do you want to visit family? There are lots of details and costs involved. When the two share the planning, she has the opportunity to make some changes that can make the travelling much nicer for both. This approach makes traveling meet her expectation P.

Sometimes you also need to visit a hospital or major medical center for yourself or your family. Who is going to do all the planning for when and then book accommodations. There can be substantial costs and time involved so this action needs to be a joint decision.

<u>Living Quarters</u>: Countryside or city? On the seashore or in the mountains? Where do you work – do you have to travel to get to your job? Is the your preferred location peaceful? What do you want – a very modest apartment, a single house, an upscale condo? What can you afford?

<u>Special Interests</u>: Would you like to live on the ski slope, near the ball park or a museum or is fishing your pleasure?

<u>Having a family</u>: Most couples would like a family of their own. That is a major decision. The first question is when. With both the guy and gal working, this means that a promotion and added duties, or travel requirements can be denied because one of you can't be there. You need

to have space for a child or children to sleep, closet space for clothes and toys and later for their hobbies and interests. As part of that you may want to wallpaper or paint the child's room.

You may have decided on a specific kind of car or vehicle you need but now rethink your choice since that vehicle is going to have to accommodate more luggage and seating room. A SUV, a van or even a small bus may be a better choice.

Keep working on your expectations: Your life is being overrun with actions that are taking place. If you want long term happiness you still have to work on negotiating your expectations.

The first six items A-E on both lists are an easy match. When item F includes cleaning the shower doors, a gal can easily persuade her guy to do so by saying that if he is doing that, she could also shower with him and he could soap up her back. That could lead to a delightful few minutes and sets the stage for frequent shower cleaning. Under these circumstances, most guys will quickly agree that item G on his list - hanging a slip or stockings to dry on a shower bar or towel rack - is just fine with him. A smart gal will just hang one or two items at a time and make that a reasonable standard action.

Getting suits etc. to the cleaner (Item H) is another easy compromise, particularly when the cleaner is close by. A plus for a gal is to ask with a smile if her guy would also take a garment or two of hers to the cleaner. That's just a trivial request so it's no problem for him.

On his list (Items I and J), she plays housemaid and that means she dumps dirty clothes in the washer, then moves them to the dryer and finally puts them back in the drawer. In real life, he maybe home and can be asked to get the clothes in the washer and later empty the laundry and put the clothes back where they belong.

High on his list are meal items K, L, and M. That means he expects his gal to do the food shopping, set the table, cook dinner and always includes his favorite foods. In real life, she would appreciate his company and help when she picks up a large bag of potatoes or other items. Hauling bags of groceries and packages of fruits and vegetables home can be difficult, especially if the gal is a small person. Once home, groceries have to be put away before she can start making meals. Sometimes his gal also has to prepare special meals for sick children or aged family. He should not hover around like a fly hunting for dinner, but lend a hand in setting the table, getting small children and relatives to the table and preparing to help cut up a roasted chicken, turkey, steak etc. Doing this answers items K and L on her list. When he sits and chats with her about what she likes to cook and her favorite recipes for items like cheesecake, pineapple-meringue upside down cake, apple pie, and different tarts, this shows an appreciation for her culinary skills. When she knits a cap or a sweater, he sees an example of craftmanship that she does it out of love for him and for her family. He would be wise to say something like 'I did not realize you were so talented'. Such thoughtful remarks answer her item M.

Like many gals she enjoys entertaining guests, especially when he lends a helping hand in planning for food and drink to be served – that is a good response to her expectation item N. Some gals have a great interest in sports but not all put pro football attendance or watching them on TV at the top of their list as many guys do. Some are fascinated by other sports such as hockey, lacrosse, tennis, golf, or skiing. There are some sports which both guys and gals find interested such as ten-pins, duck pins, square dancing or ballroom dancing. These mutually interesting sports are a good response to her expectation O.

<u>Educating your children</u>: 529 plans are ways to save that allow you to put money aside for a child's education. Earnings on your 529 savings are not subject to federal taxes and that tax free status goes for up to some 23 thousand dollars. If you have several children, each can

have their own 529 plan. Some states will allow a deduction on their state income tax return for some part of your payments into the 529 plan,. For specifics on your state, check with a local tax expert or your state tax office.

529 funds can be used for most kinds of education. Training costs can be held down if you have access to a local community college and most states charge less if you live in the state. If your child has special talents or is gifted. he/she often needs to go to a center of excellence which understands how to handle such children who frequently need extra training in developing social skills. Costs to attend one of these centers can be substantial. One difficulty for many parents is to handle the cost and the time to travel between home and the center.

<u>Family finances</u>: Unfortunately, almost no high schools and few colleges go into any depth on how to handle family finances. An easy way to get into planning finances is to look at short term items for the current week, then lay out a list of items that you would typically pay in a month or two, and then then try to put together a list that goes for a year or perhaps two. In the current week's budget, you need to figure out how much cash you will need for groceries, gasoline, what you are spending on entertainment and what's left over. Don't forget amounts you spent on credit cards and checks you

may have written. With luck, you will have some cash left over that you can save each week. Even a small thing like buying coffee from a vendor can chew up your free cash.

Putting together these the three lists as EXCEL worksheets is a good approach because you can easily add items you forgot while you are putting in your best estimates of the costs. It is good idea to put the date you prepare a worksheet and its computer file name on the top of the work sheet so finding and then updating that worksheet is much faster. You can also use the updated worksheet when talking to a financial advisor or a CPA who is doing your tax returns.

Taxes: If you are a salaried wage earner you will notice that your payroll department deducts taxes from each paycheck. You still need to fill out your federal and state tax returns. To do this, some people use a software tax program such as Turbo Tax or H&R Block and others go to a local tax preparer or a CPA (a Certified Public Accountant).

Life Insurance: In many cases, a guy is the breadwinner in a family. Often, a gal may be a second active worker. A breadwinner should realize that he/she is going to have to buy at least basic life insurance. If you are going to have a family soon, get a clause in your policy (a policy rider) that allows you to increase the policy size without having to face a medical exam. Having a child means that the policy has to be large enough to bring up the child for some years.

Since starting salaries may be low, so buying much less expensive term insurance may be a better choice than buying whole life. The insurance agent you deal with should be able to explain these choices. Some agents who are especially knowledgeable in life insurance earn a highly regarded professional designation as a CLU. A CLU is a Certified Life Underwriter.

Home Owners Insurance: You need insurance for your home. Most basic policies also offer different features. The first piece of that insurance is for fire. Does that fire policy pay for renting quarters elsewhere? What about replacing clothes and appliances? Will they get you the same or better appliances? It helps greatly if you have pictures of fancy costly clothing and any receipts for expensive TVs and computer equipment.

If you live in a low-lying area where flooding may occur you also need flood insurance that pays for replacing floor, walls, etc. Some states offer this type of insurance. This kind of insurance is often purchased for beachfront properties

Burial Costs: Most young families ignore this item. If you have older parents, they may need to plan ahead for this so you don't get unexpectedly stuck with a big bill. Total costs for a funeral can range all over the lot. Cremation normally the lowest because there is embalming, no casket, no grave site to buy or to dig and no grave marker. Costs for a funeral would include such things as having a priest, an iman or rabbi giving a short eulogy at the grave site.

When the deceased is going to be buried there are costs for opening and closing the grave and cost to have a flat, grave marker - typically a bronze plaque - placed at the gravesite. Large monuments can have costs ranging into the thousands. That's not all. Graveyard operators want the graves clean and neat so they can be visited at any time so they strongly prefer you pay a one-time charge for perpetual care. If you are fortunate, your parents paid many of the costs before they died.

For more information: Having a happy life and a family is most everyone's dream. It typically involves marriage and raising successful children. Raising children and coping with common problems is addressed in several very readable books just published through AMAZON and also available through BARNES & NOBLE. Go to your computer browser and type in: www.henryhpetersohn.com to get a quick look at 'A Father's Handbook for Raising Children' (a 303 page hardback) and shorter printed books including KILL STRESS and Love is in the Air.

About the Author

Henry H. Petersohn

A Ph.D is a research and teaching degree. Petersohn previously taught business management and statistics and has written on computer topics. He personally had to undergo serious cardiac surgery and a stressful recovery and that involved Johns Hopkins and the Med-Star Hospital in DC. He also had to deal with more than two dozen family medical issues that pushed him into working with London's National Health System and Venice's Mesre as well as the Cleveland Clinic in Cleveland and St. Joseph's in Phoenix. He was drawn into extensive medical research as family issues became serious which spurred a deep interest in researching medical journals and reports from sources such as NIH, Johns Hopkins, UCLA, Emory University, and the MAYO Clinic.

www.ingramcontent.com/pod-product-compliance
Lightning Source LLC
Chambersburg PA
CBHW040728120726
48010CB00001B/49